Strangers' Voices in My Head

A Journey Through What Made Me Who I Am from My Mind

SHAWN P. LEHTO

PAGE PUBLISHING, INC.
New York, NY

First originally published by Page Publishing, Inc. 2018

ISBN 978-1-64350-145-1 (Paperback)
ISBN 978-1-64350-146-8 (Digital)

Printed in the United States of America

Contents

Foreword

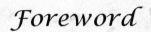

These words are dedicated to those who have believed in me from the beginning; those who inspired me to continue writing, even when I felt that my words just weren't good enough.

The things I write come from the *voices* in my head. I hear the words when I am finally at ease and alone with my own thoughts. I write what I do, and most have a meaning I think only I can understand. Hopefully, others can get what I say.

I can't thank everyone enough.

The Stranger

Standing in a crowd, but all alone
Just another face that nobody knows
He stands there with no purpose
Just being there is reason enough
No one knows and no one cares
Who he is or what he does
Just another stranger waiting there

What's his purpose, where does he come from
Just more questions that have been asked
about the man who is all alone
Never seen with anybody
But always seen with somebody
Can't keep up with him
Because he is never there

He isn't anyone important
Never done anything special
No known hero is he
He's just an average person
Who is always somewhere
But is never to be found

The best way to describe him would be a John Doe
He doesn't have a name that anybody knows
Nobody asks question because nobody cares
He's just a stranger off the street
With no special place to go
So he wanders off aimlessly
With no specific cause at all

This person is someone with whom we are all acquainted
    with
Because deep down inside, he is you and me

We are all like the stranger
At times in our life
We just can't fight it
For it's a part of being alive

We all confess that to an extent
That there will always be a stranger
That lives somewhere inside our souls
Just waiting to bust out to be all alone

Seasons

Crisp and clear is the air
Nothing else to do, so we just stand there
The colors around are a fiery red
We make the fallen leaves our bed

We seem to thrive this time of year
When family will come from far and near
This is what we like to call
The first season of autumn or fall

Cold and harsh is the wind
This time of year is not our friend
Rain and snow fall from the sky
Which, in turn, causes us to run and hide

There is not too much for us to do
Until this time of year passes through
There must be a very good reason
That not many people enjoy the winter season

Bright and sunny is the sky
Love shines brightly in everyone's eyes
Flowers grow in fields of green
The earth itself smells fresh and clean

Everyone around celebrates with joy
Like a child with a brand-new toy
This time of year can cause us to sing
The wonderful season we call the spring

Hot and humid is the night
No sign of relief is in sight
The beach seems the logical place to go
While we all hope soon for rain or snow

We run around without any care in the world
And all the boys are searching for the girls
There is no way to call this time a bummer
The fourth and final season, we refer to as summer

The four seasons shall never change
And the order they arrive you can't rearrange
The four seasons we shall always call
Winter, summer, spring, and fall

28 May 1993

Ghosts

A ghost from my past comes back to haunt me
As I close my eyes, it's the only thing I ever see
The memories they bring up should be kept from my view
But after seeing their faces, there isn't anything that I can do

I thought they were gone and the nightmares would end
I don't want them around, not even as a long-lost friend
I wish they would go and cease to exist
Because the pain they caused is something that will never
  be missed

Go away and please never return
Then all the old memories I shall soon burn
Leave this instant, and this time make it last
Forever stay as you were—a ghost from my past

The Way I Feel

I have a lot of things weighing on my mind
But the words to describe them are so hard to find
I wouldn't even know just where I should start
Should I go with what's in my head or begin with my heart

I suppose I should start with the thoughts in my head
For this is where I store all my feelings of dread
I am so confused, my thoughts are jumbled into a mess
I can't take much more, though I surely could use much less

I don't know if I can keep it inside me much longer
But I know I have to, for it will only make me stronger
I have to tell someone before it makes me crack
Because it will help to get this monkey off my back

I do think now, my head was the wrong place to go
So I shall look to my heart, that's where my feelings do grow
I can't understand what exactly it is I feel
For my heart is the place that would know what is real

Why do I always feel this terrible guilt
Is it because of the walls I have consistently built
I let no one inside up until now
I sit off to the side and continue to cower

I have been hurt and my heart has been broke
So when I think about it, I begin to choke
I try to hold back the tears before they start to fall
But somehow they break through my impenetrable wall

It's not something that I am proud to say
And I hate that I still have to feel this way
I don't think that I will ever be able to commit
To let someone inside, then on my feelings they spit

A blow like that would be my end
And then it would take more than a friend
To help me recover from the impending doom
Then a new wall I build, leaving absolutely no room

I'll close up my heart 'til the day that I die
Never to let someone ever get inside
I'll leave this place the way I came
Because my life will never be the same

A Question of Why

How much more can one heart take
Before it suffers its final break
I was as courteous as I could be
But in the end, she still left me

Everything I did was strictly for her
So why do I feel like I still got burned
Am I going to live my life always playing the fool
Or will somebody please explain to me all the rules

I did some things I will forever regret
The only reason I did, was that I became upset
By my side she was safe from all of life's harms
Yet in the end she left in another man's arms

I didn't do much wrong that I could see
Is this the way my life will forever be
I keep telling myself to seal up that door
Never to let anyone in forevermore

Like an idiot, I will still give them a chance
And with my mind, they do their little dance
They will build me up and make me believe
I am their only one, then leave me to grieve

I want to be more than just their plaything
But I guess it will only be just my dream
I hope to wake up one day from my inner nightmare
To find someone real still standing right there

For now I will let time continue to drift on by
Yet you will never witness me cry
I will lose my temper, I may stay mad
Just to mask my feeling very sad

People always say that it gets better over time
Meanwhile you are paying for someone else's crime
One day my heart will begin to mend
But will never be the same again

Left Clueless

A fleeting glance across the room
A faceless expression within the gloom
Trying to figure out exactly who you are
While I sit lonely and deserted inside this bar

Not having any hint or possible clue
Still trying to remember what exactly I must do
Always searching high as well as low
I will never give up until I absolutely do know

Chasing a face without a name
Suddenly realizing that I shall never be the same
I refuse to give up, nor shall I quit this race
knowing the answers are somewhere in this place

Come back and give me a clue this time
So the mystery of this won't only be mine
It's obvious that you know all about me
Give me a chance for my head to be free

A glimpse of hope is all I seek
So that I can become stronger and not feel as weak
The answers I seek shall soon be found
If not from the air, then buried underground

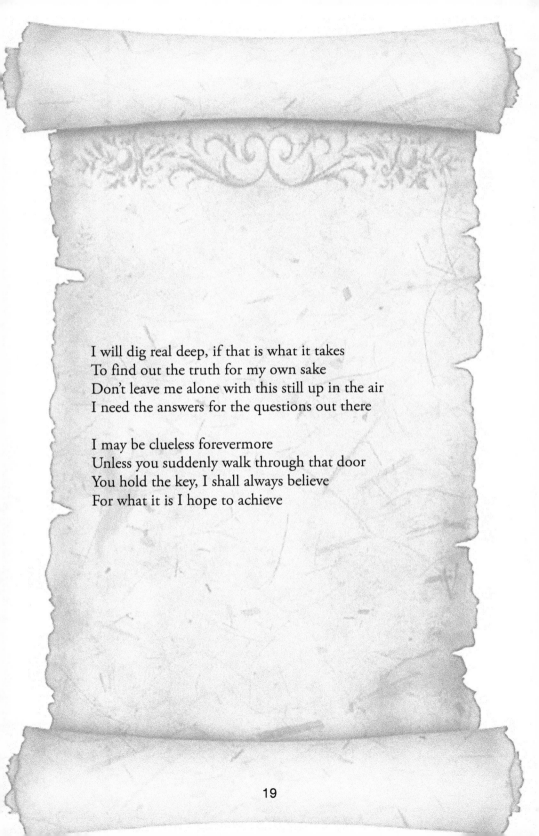

I will dig real deep, if that is what it takes
To find out the truth for my own sake
Don't leave me alone with this still up in the air
I need the answers for the questions out there

I may be clueless forevermore
Unless you suddenly walk through that door
You hold the key, I shall always believe
For what it is I hope to achieve

The Nameless Man
(The Stranger: Part Two)

The nameless man still waits around
Totally unaware of the growing crowd
They can't fully see him, but they know he is there
Just feeling his presence, though not sure exactly where

Feeling left out, he walks off alone
No one knows how much his pain has grown
He longs for something, but not sure what
So he stands alone on the corner, seemingly stuck in a rut

He asks himself a question, not really sure why
Is it the wind that makes him start to cry
Doubting everything, he leaves this place
Completely unaware of his importance to the human race

Soon he will leave without a definitive plan
Only knowing forever that he is the nameless man
Time flies on, but he doesn't care
Always standing around, though never really there

One day he will forever leave
Yet no one will ever care enough to truly grieve
Just another soul left in the dust
A replacement will come, it is a must

You never know who it is going to be
Look around and they are the ones you will never see
Stuck to roam upon this land
He is the next one branded the nameless man

Road to a New Life

The roads you have traveled are winding away
Looking back, all you see is your yesterday
The steps you have taken are wearing you down
And every crossing you pass only leads back to town

Back to the place you have remembered from before
Never to go back is what you swore
So you walk on by to leave it in the dust
To start a brand-new life, that is a must

Lonely roads are forsaken, the world drifts on by
There is nothing between you but the path and the sky
You will continue to wander until you find a new life
Without all the pain, the sorrow, and the strife

You come upon a new town, so into it you go
But the first thing you witness is somebody you know
You turn your back and walk out of this place
Never to look at another empty space

Into the sunset you go, the whole world left to see
Only you can make it to be as it should be
You will find a new home where you shall fit in
Then with your new life you shall begin

Ten Steps of Life

Sleepless
Lying there in a haze
Restless
Walking around in a daze
Helpless
Being there by yourself
Useless
You place your life upon a shelf
Loneliness
No one around to lend a hand
Madness
You have taken all that you can stand
Bitterness
Resentment toward all those around
Quietness
You want to leave without making a sound
Peacefulness
There is nothing left that you can say
Happiness
What you are hoping to achieve at the end of the day

Remember Them

Remember them for all they have done
Not only the good or all the fun
A good example they may not always set
But then you don't know what you should expect

Try to remember all that you have heard
Then maybe their lessons will somehow be learned
You may not be sure if it's right for you
The things they teach will always ring true

When they have gone on to a better place
The truths they speak can help the entire human race
You may not have believed when they were alive
So listen up when they die
The choices they made are reflected in your moves
What else is there for you to lose

Remember the paths that they took
Follow their lead, but always look
For something better that lies ahead
Leave a legacy of your own when you are dead

Give to others those things you knew
Don't be selfish with it, let others learn from it too
Take it all in, one step at a time
With the knowledge you have built up, to the top you
will climb

Don't grieve for them, but take the lead
For what you have learned, others shall soon also need
Things will change if you take the chance today
Just remember the words you have heard them say

14 April 1995

The One

They say the one will come around someday
But will it happen before I'm old and gray
Must I stand at the end of the line
Only to reach the front and have run out of time

Will they tell me I have run out of luck
That eternal solitude is where I will be stuck
Can I break down the wall and escape from this jail
Or am I stuck here forever, unable to afford my bail

Is the price too high for the one to pay
So they bid adieu and walk away
Am I asking too much for a bit of happiness
If so I will lower my price to get out of this mess

They say the one will come, I do know
Yet until that time, I'll just watch the show
I'll sit and learn just what to do
To get the one they say for me is you

Alternate Life

Stranded on the road away from all you know
A place where your thoughts are free to roam
Among the shadows you find your place
Taken away from all members of the human race

You now remember things you have forgotten before
Somehow they appear and continue to grow
Alone with yourself you begin to seek
Those things that will make your life complete

The answers to which you will faithfully serve
Then someone comes along and throws you a curve
You suddenly lose all train of thought
But with this delay, more time you have bought

To rearrange your mind and set it straight
Though what is to come, you must now patiently wait
You're not too sure what will happen next
The one thing you know, it's for the best

Eventually, you will do what you feel is right
And your escape from it all is definitely within sight

Soon you will go back to a populated land
Once again you must deal with the common man
You'll go with whatever your mind has set
Then everything else you'll eventually forget

Vision

I have a vision trapped deep within my mind
But the clarity is off, so the truth is hard to find
I search to see what's really out there
The investigation grows cold, with no clues to spare

What lies inside the depths of one's soul
To make them spin as if out of control
A determination to make all around them right
Yet their focus is relegated to a nonjudgmental sight

For if you open your eyes and gaze all about
Eventually those mysteries will show themselves out
To try to disguise what you truly will feel
Is like trying to believe that Santa is real

The haze in your memories can become more clear
If you don't think too much and let it appear
The moment you focus all the energy you can
The more you can figure out exactly where you stand

It's all in your heart, your soul, and your head
So unwind your fears and lay them to bed
As soon as you relax, the clearer you shall see
That the vision so hazy could only be me

Child
(Ashlie's Poem)

A child was born six years ago today
To bring about hope and joy in her own way
With bright, shining eyes and a smile so gay
With warmth and love in her heart to play

With blond curly hair and eyes so blue
An innocence grows with a heart so true
Shy she may seem when you first do appear
Stick around to watch her fears disappear

The laughter that comes from a silly little word
To tears she will cry from an unforeseen hurt
A kiss on the cheek and all is well
A hug from her arms puts you under her spell

To sit back and watch this young child play
Or simply join in and you will be swept away
To make-believe lands where dreams will abound
To the mysteries of life, those lost and found

Every day an adventure from within her mind
It all becomes new to her, what we all have left behind
To witness a life through a child's young eyes
And with each new discovery, we are filled with surprise

I now sit back, for I soon shall know
That the best thing in life is to watch my young niece grow

Choices and Roads

As time starts slipping by, we ponder what we have not
But really how much left have we got
We wander about with our heads in the clouds
Not ever really noticing the life that's around

We make the same mistakes time and again
Have we really ever learned from them, my friend
We say some things we can never hold true
It's in our nature to see it all come through

To cross those paths that stand in our way
Never really sure the price we have to pay
To travel the road not ventured upon
And think our dreams will never be gone

Taking a chance with what we have to give
Is not always the smartest way to live
You may not choose the door that's right
Yet if it's your decision, then for it you must fight

I have chosen my roads with no set plan
To prove to myself and not others that I am a man
The way I have picked is the right way for me
To venture out to the world so that I may see

I may not be the person others have had in mind
But with this decision I made, they shall stand behind
I choose this place, for I know it to be true
I have chosen the way that leads straight to you

So accept me for the mistakes I have made
And forgive me for my past before I lie in my grave
Take me for the person you shall never want to leave
For when my time finally comes, you shall never have to
      grieve

We will live out our lives the way we want to
The decision is ours, both me and you
Accept what you can and walk away
For then by your side, I shall forever stay

Stormy Seas

Adrift somewhere at sea, yet out of the storm
Searching for passages is not out of the norm
Waiting for life to come to rescue me
But finding no answers for life to let me be

Floating upon every wave after wave
Is there nothing left out here for me to now save
Crashing upon the rocky old shore
With nothing to guide me but tales of distant lore

I seek only answers from this cold, watery past
For will the memories I savor be forever to last
Can I escape the reality I have been thrown in
Or be lost from land and soaked to the skin

As I float upon the ocean, toward its unending path
For when she's awoken, you succumb to her wrath
One moment she's calm and blissfully so
Next moment you hang on for the life you love and know

You are guided along from the stars up above
Knowing somewhere out there is the only one you love
You glance toward the horizon to stare at the sky
Alone in your head, you still question why

What set you adrift toward this course you are on
And will the end come soon, or has the future now gone
You have checked out the maps, sure of where you must go
But in the end, you wind up following only what you know

Relying on things that only you can trust
To survive mother earth and her rage you must
Traveling along with plans set firmly in stone
Knowing that in the end, you were never alone

Setting sail upon her stormy old seas
Knowing you remain safe from old enemies
It may take a while for your journey to end
No matter where you stop, always do you find a friend

Stages

Lifeless
Standing in the middle of your life's real despair
Still wondering how the hell you ended up there
Is there a chance to regain what you certainly have lost
Or would it be too much for you to pay what it shall cost

Loveless
So now you have found out what it's like to be alone in
        the end
With all your doubts, you can no longer pretend
You have given all your heart can afford to pay out
But a life with a significant other is not what it's about

Thoughtless
You have always done things without a helping hand
When you have had troubles, where do your friends now
        stand
You never truly cared what others have thought about you
When asked by them for help, you knew what you had
        to do
You walk away with your nose stuck up in the air
It didn't concern you, so why should you care

Trust
Your heart has been broken so many times before
You don't feel you can handle it to happen anymore
So you had shut yourself down from letting anyone in
Now to find someone, you aren't sure where you are to begin

Honesty
You have heard the lies spew forth from their mouths
That you just can't believe anything they do talk about
They tell you one thing and then come back to say
You have heard me wrong, what kind of games do they play
A chance to redeem themselves in your eyes
But the doubts appear if it's the truth or all lies

Faith
To forget all you have seen or done in your past
To rely on others to help you achieve your dreams at last
To hold on to someone without a single care
To blindly grab hold, though you're not certain they actu-
     ally are there

These patterns of life are what make up who you are
So trust that you will be guided from near to far
Take the hand of the one only you are able to see
Understand that life is what you make it out to be
Opportunities arise when you least expect them to come
     to pass
But if you let go, to then hold on, they will be there,
     forever to last

Journey

Giving in and pondering what life is all about
Yet standing alone on the sidelines, I'm left with no doubt
A shadow falls across the path I shall lead
To find out what it is I soon shall need

Awash in the memories, I find no way that seems clear
Am I now farther away from what I believed was so near
Have I grazed my own path and thus chosen my road
Leaving myself no possible way to burden this load

Am I stuck in the present, destined to always relive my past
Have the mistakes I made been set to forever last
A tear in my eye to wash away the dust
To now go on, certainly I must

I start on through the mist and the haze
To sort out my life while still trapped in its maze
A guiding star won't lead me toward the very end
And no stranger's hand to assist me where I shall find no
    friend

Choices were made, and the roads have been set
From recalling of memories and the doubts filled with
    regrets
I walk away without a real reason to start
But to lead me to you and the journey from my heart

I have packed up my belongings and then given away
Everything not now needed, for here I cannot stay
This journey was spoken to me in a dream
Now it's up to me to decipher what all it will mean

When the road comes to where it shall lead me
I look back to where I have been, yet I still am unable to
    see
I know I have traveled a million miles or two
Yet in the end, my journey always ends up coming right
    back to you

Broken Glass

Broken glass is all I see
Nothing left for you but me
Everything that could not be
Is all I hold in my memory

All I take I cannot hold
The feelings have died, my heart's been sold
So take a chance with all you are told
My love for you will never grow old

All that I have and all that I know
All I can give to you, I will now show
Everything I possess is yours to take
Before the glass in front of you breaks
You cannot see until you open your eyes
What stands here before you is without a disguise
Who can he be and where shall he lay
For the person before you won't ever go away

I left here with nothing to leave for you behind
A feeling for you could not be so kind
Whatever you want has been gifted to you
Nothing is left for me that I can do
Take what is yours, but please leave the rest
I have given unto you all the very best

Your memory shall still burn inside
My love for you I can never hide
I will bow down to your loving grace
For one last glance of your angelic face

Take your time to remember this
I will always remember the very last kiss
With your hand inside mine
We will take this trip for one last time
Down the road with you I go
Until we play just one last show

Eternal love is what we got
One more chance for one last shot
With you and me, I just can't end
All my love to you I'll send

The broken glass is just a sign
Of memories shattered somewhere in time
So take what you can, but go with care
For the shards that remain will show that we have always
    been there

Familiarity

Can you ever leave a place you don't believe you have ever
been
Yet it all seems familiar from what you have seen
It's like walking around and you know exactly what's there
But in the back of your mind it's really nowhere

In the faces of those that are lingering about
The same questions are painted, can we ever get out
We see each other out upon the street
We've spoken before, but did we ever really meet

The same routines from day to day
Go to this place and that, yet it's here that we stay
Some will venture down a different road
Yet we all come back, it has been foretold

You pack up your things, ready to finally be free
But you turn right around and it's the same places that
you see
You know you have been traveling, seeming to have gone
far
Yet you blink your eyes and here you still are

Like a baby bird, you need to leave the nest
And like the prodigal son, you come back with the rest
Maybe the comfort of it all keeps you so near
To strike out on your own, you need to alleviate that fear

The world is the same wherever you may go
So sit back, relax, and just follow the flow
You cannot run through, though you may try
The burdens you carry are the main reason why

To live in a place you have lived in before
Yet when you open your eyes, you see so much more
You think you have gone to a place so new
But when you think about it, it's only that way to you

The Seeker

Like living in a vacuum with the suction cut off
I'm not really sure what I have done or if it's enough
I've tried to do the best I can
To grow in this world to become a better man

I accept the things that I have done
with those mistakes I have chosen the path I am now on
I see the way I am going to go
But it's the finish that's ahead I really want to know

The signs all point to the truth that I seek
Though the answers I get are for the strong and not the weak
I travel this life with no known bounds
Yet my existence is needed, for I'm alive and still aboveground

So smile when you gaze upon the scars on my face
For the scars are inside their own hiding place
Reliving the memories of a once-joyful youth
For only in those moments will you find your inner truth

A day like this is abundant with tears
Though through all this, you escape what was not very clear
To walk alone in this vastly distant place
Your mind reveals the emptiness of this long-forgotten space

Wishes

To be with you from this day on
To hear you speak, it's just like a song
To let you know I shall always be true
And never to know any sorrow from you

To always be there, right by your side
To never again with my feelings do hide
To let you know I shall never exist
Until I feel your tender kiss

To walk with you, hand in hand
Across the beach, or through desert sand
To show you all that's true and right
To have you never leave my sight

To be with you until my dying day
To hear you say I do, in that loving way
To make you forget all that's wrong
To remain the one who shall be strong

Never to make you shed a tear
To protect you from all that you fear
To never argue but pacify
To let you see I am the only guy

To always give and never take
And with your heart I shall never break
These are the wishes I hope will come true
To end it with these three words—"I love you"

Soul-Searching

When I start to look inside myself, I'm scared of what I see
Of the person in front of my eyes, could that really be me
I have to press deeper to find the answers I seek
To make up for all the times I found myself weak

All the things I've done and said to make you go away
The way I feel when you're gone, the times I let you stray
I can't take back the wrong I've done, for it's my ego that
    did lead
But you have to know, down in your heart, you're all I'll
    ever need

I must continue to search my soul
And let the emotions take control
If I don't, then I shall take
All that's left for my heart to break
You must truly understand
That in this case, you have the upper hand
I have to find a way back to your loving heart
So inside myself is where I need to start

The times I've cried and broken down
When life was the lowest I have ever found
To the times my elation was at its peak
Those are all the things I must continue to seek

I look at all the times we've shared, and I never should
        have let you go
But then I see the pain I've caused, and now I truly know
Can I take back all the things I've done, is there ever really
        a chance
I'm beginning to think it is gone, now that you've taken
        your stance

Looking around and finding no answers I seek tonight
I start to feel that something about this just isn't right
I let the worries turn into doubt
And all I want to do is scream and shout

There must be answers hidden there, the reasons that it
        must be
Something that must surface, so I can truly see
The words I have said, to those I have hid, deep within
        my mind
Some are better left unspoken, for not always were they kind

I leave with you this one last thought to sleep upon and
        dream
How would life be without me, could it be as bad as my
        mind will make it seem
I continue to look inside myself and not know if it all is true
I know that in the very end, it can only lead me back to you

Scared Speechless

Can I open my mouth to convey what I have to say
Or will I let you get up and then walk away
Will I ever know exactly what I have to do
So what I'm asking is can I be me without you

There are so many words that I need to speak
Yet when it comes down to it, I am so very weak
My mouth drops open, but no words can I utter
It's like my mind has melted, like a hot pan of butter

Give me the courage to help me get through this state of
    mind
For without the ability to speak, I may as well be also blind
Because if I don't see you, it makes it easier to talk
It's the sight of your beauty that forces my voice to
    become blocked
Someday I'll break the spell you put me under
Then my voice shall ring forth, louder than the thunder

Opportunities Arise

The one you always dream about
So close you feel no need to shout
Within a foot, though not that near
The one your heart holds so dear

Then all at once our eyes do meet
You sense your heart has skipped a beat
As you sit there, no words do you say
Another golden opportunity has been wasted away

Your soul was ready, but you were not
This could have been, and it was your one perfect spot
To speak the words rustling around inside your brain
Now the chance has been flushed slowly down the drain

As she leaves, she says goodbye
Suddenly you wish that you could die
You have blown the chance that you once had
So all you're left to feel is sad

You will try again, or so you do think
For another opportunity shall arise one week
You'll voice the words, your sorrow shall end
Not only will she be a beautiful dream, but now, more
than a friend

The Good Disguise

It's true what they say, the rain does hide your tears
It's also helpful to hide your fears
When you are bundled up, your head bent down
No one can notice your well-placed frown

The tears will flow that no one can see
The rain is what they think it will be
You will hide it well so cry away
Never let it be any different today

Walk around and do what you will
No one can change the things you feel

The rain will always be good to hide
All the sorrow you feel inside
Go on out into the pouring rain
Don't worry for others will never see your pain

When the sun comes out, put a smile on your face
Just remember your sadness will soon take its place
When the clouds start to form and the drops do fall
From the depths of your soul, the sorrow will crawl

Searching for Something

Still wilder than a western wind
You write it out, the message you send
The words you speak are not all that clear
It's as though you are still not standing here

Roaming about looking for more
Something better than you have had before
A different setting from where you are
It's not exactly near, but it's not that far

Open yourself up and take a look around
Or the place you seek will never be found
Everywhere you go, you will find something wrong
The travels you started have lasted too long

You will find the spot if you open your eyes
It's not really hidden or in a disguise
It is much easier to find if you look hard enough
Just let yourself go, it's really not that tough

Keep searching around for what it's worth
The time you seek is at your birth
Where all was right and much too real
Happiness and content were all you could feel

You will look for something like that feeling again
You won't really find it, for you don't know where to begin
Give up that search and live for today
Because you will never know another way

Oceans

The grains on the beach, like the sands of time
Restlessly sitting there with no reason or rhyme
Getting tossed in the air, they slowly drift away
Where they are to land, no one can ever really say

Waves come to show and then do they recede
Like the minutes on a clock we so desperately need
Back and forth, they rush to see
Where they will stop to somehow be free

Light from the sun beating down upon our back
To put color on our skin, but not as an attack
We relish the heat from the unseen rays
Until darkness sets in and beckons us away

Kids run around with nary a care
For school is out and it's fun out there
Collecting strange shells they find in the surf
Maybe taking a home from the sand crabs' turf

Laughter and shouts of joy are so often heard
Yet rarely will you listen to an angry spoken word
There's something about racing through life in the sun
It seems the ocean is the place for all fun

Although there are many others around, they seem to be
    in a world of their own
You do what you must for out here your spirits have grown

At nighttime it sets a special mood it does seem
There to walk on its surface with the person of your dreams
Hand in hand so close to the shore
To get your feet wet seems to enhance it that much more

Staring up at the moon, you realize a change
How different it all seems, it's all so strange
It is much more quiet than during the day
But I think you agree, somehow it is so much better that
    way

Reasonable Doubts

Can you ever miss what was never truly there
And without really feeling it, can you know that they ever
   did care
When you are left in the dark, can a memory be hard to bear
Or will the end result be something that you can never
   share

Wallowing in the sorrow—of what, you're not sure
Try as you must, for that there is no known cure
Did the thoughts ever exist or were they just part of a dream
Yet inside your heart, to those thoughts you must cling

Trapped in abyss with no proven way out
So you search for a meaning, but on grows your doubt
You think you may have found a reason to go
But when those moments occur, your fear does now show

On the outside you showcase both sorrow and grit
Alone on the inside you feel as though you have been hit
You trudge through the day accomplishing what you can
And the rest of the world will only see the *real* man

At times like these you begin to reflect on it all
And realize somewhere along the way, you started to fall
You can't really pinpoint the time that it did start
But you suddenly lost track of the joy in your heart

You can't replace the sands in the glass
Nor can you throw them away, they are what is your past
You can't turn it over and start all anew
So now in your mind, you ask what is there to do

You relinquish your hold on all that you feel
You don't want to endure all the remorse that is real
So here with your thoughts, you sit and then dwell
For never knowing how to deal with your personal hell

The days will pass, and you will go on
Not ever physically there to say exactly where it has gone
And if you have never felt you lost your place in this earth
Somehow you are mistaken, you lost it at your birth

Enslaved

Take these shackles off my wrist
Just do it now, for this I must insist
I stayed your slave for much too long
And when I'm free, I shall remain strong

I've taken all that you can give
But now it's time for me to live
To be the person I need to be
Without your influence, so set me free

You have struggled to keep me in your control
To manipulate my mind to keep your hold
I always thought that you were right
But within my own eyes, I have seen the light

I have taken all that I possibly can
From now on, with my own two feet, I shall stand
The games were fun when we had our start
It slowly turned bad when you had my heart

Unleash the chains that bind me still
And let me live my own free will
The physical bonds no longer remain
It's the emotional ones that still bring on the pain

You have heard my pleas, so make your call
And end my sentence, once and for all
To be bound to you, I no longer care
I only wish to leave you standing there

No longer with my voice will you constrict
Sometimes it's worse than being an addict
You no longer have control, your life is a mess
Just cut the damn chains, so in peace I shall soon rest

Personal Musings of a Convoluted Mind

They say as you go through life, you experience many things
Some joy, some pain, some discontent, and some power
    it will bring
You don't have a way to truly comprehend
How you ever could justify the meaning to the end

Throughout my existence I have accomplished some goals
But in my heart I know I will never get to reach them all
I have striven to be the best I could
Yet I know, in some ways, I am not as I should

Many things I have yet to experience in life
So what holds me back but the fear I hold inside
I cannot change the wrongs that I have done
Or take back the pain that I may have caused to someone

I can only look forward to try to better my path
Yet the farther ahead I look, I always envision what was
    my past
How do you go from where you are
To moving forward yet ending up like a backward-facing
    car

I have some friends and family that I love
But at times I don't feel like that is enough
Why do I seek for more than what I have in front of me
It doesn't seem to be a connected circle I see

I show my joy to all I know
Yet if you really know the truth, my true heart will always
    show
I wear it on my proverbial sleeve
Just read the signs, it shines like neon, I do believe

As we come upon the season of joy and cheer
I realize my ways of thinking are not going to be that clear
I never will say out loud how it really is
So read between the lines, and you will understand the
    gist

I'll crack the jokes, impersonate, and be your fool
Just because that's how I handle a life so cruel
Take these thoughts for what they are
I am writing because it helps me deal with this life from
    afar

I express things better with a well-written word
Maybe it's the fact I can see it makes is seem more real
    than just being heard
Everyone has demons they just can't overcome
Mine has taken hold and won't be undone

I like to think I spread happiness wherever I go
If not I shall work on rewriting my show
I hold true to the fact, I will always be me
And maybe that's the person you all do perceive

Who are we really when we glance at ourselves at night
Are we the person we envisioned we would be as a child
Do we ever really know if we have become what it is we
    wanted for us
Or is it always a longer road that we roam upon and never
    trust

I take this journey through my life without a guide
Yet without the wisdom I seek, I am wasting away my time
Go on as I must for the betterment I do seek
Yet slowly I shall go, for in the end of it all, I grow a little
    weak

Be true to who you are, for life can be a pain
Enjoy what you can, for sometimes you deal with only
    more rain
Some sun will shine on you for a minute or two
And maybe that's all you need to become the one you
    wish to be you

Schizophrenia

Thoughts and voices running throughout my brain
Destined, I believe, to make me insane
Words I can't seem to grip so that I may write them down
They get tossed in the air, yet none will fall to the ground

I attempt to regrab those still within my reach
And watch the others float away, never to be written in
    my speech
I gather those that do remain into a tightly wound bunch
So I can sort them into a song that will really pack a punch

I hear these voices in my head
It makes me realize that I'm still not dead
I see the words as I write them out
And come to know that this is what it's all about
I don't have to struggle, nor should I ever fear
The meaning of it all shall soon be so clear

I started this day with no reasoning or clue
But as soon as I awoke, my thoughts turned to you
The sounds creeping in were distinguished and bold
Yet putting them together suddenly made me feel so cold

I try to ignore them, but they won't go away
They just fester and multiply, until my mind goes astray
So many thoughts go racing around inside
From them I can never run, nor can I ever hide

Schizophrenia is a madness, or so I have heard
It controls you every moment, you are unable to say a word
You think you can put it all under control
But eventually you lose that battle, your senses will soon
    dull

Sometimes the voices are helpful, for they helped create
    this rhyme
For all the words that were wasted, I can't give them any
    of my time
I fear for the future, if it ever takes complete hold
Just know that schizophrenia leaves us never younger,
    only old

Undenied

Unbridled, unbroken, unwilling, untrue
With only the misfortune of not knowing what to do
Unless you are not opposed to having the cure
All you have is the reason to recognize all that's pure

Undaunted by the task and goals that you set
Forever with the promise to give only what you get
To struggle with the choices, to do what is right
Yet in whose vision of serenity can you place it within
    your sight

Who is to guide you on the path to your gain
Who, besides yourself, shall set forth to carry this burden
    of pain
Whenever you venture out on paths unknown
Do you allow their guidance to be all you have until you
    have grown

Can you break from the rituals practiced many eons ago
Then with the knowledge you gain, to whom with it shall
    you now bestow
Keep it written in stone for others to read
Or proclaim it out loud to those with whom you have
    disagreed

No obvious decision can be made in spite
Or how you govern who is wrong in this fight
Unbloodied, unscathed, unfortunate, unmade
You only move forward when you have nothing you've
    saved

Untested is how you travel through life
Taking the easy way out to hopefully endure the monu-
    mental strife
You've listened, you've read, you've researched and still
You've come to the realization that it's all up to your own
    stubborn will

Unbecoming a human to give up the easy road
You travel on restlessly, shouldering the unbearable load
Without a thought or fear as to what may come next
Is the unanswerable question to the struggle for which
    you test

Uncertain Certainty

What have I done, where have I gone wrong
I've tried as hard as I could, yet still feel as though I don't
belong
I give a strong heart to those that matter and a stronger
one to those that don't
Yet when I attempt to get ahead, it seems that I only fall
back to "I know I won't"

Putting on a face of happiness and joy
Only brings me back to the feelings I want to now destroy
Pushing forward through the day, I feel redemption at last
It can only bring back memories of mistakes from my past

I'm lost for an explanation of how to break free from this
path
Yet the ones who were there to guide me can only sit back
and stifle a laugh
Is this existence merely a test from which I am set up to fail
Or is the answers I seek somewhere along this winding,
uncharted, desolate trail

Giving only the reserves I planned to utilize for myself
Have I forsaken my demons, to be used for truth that lies
softly in my personal mental hell

I wander along with absolutely no clear direction to set forth
To seek the fortunes of others that lie no gentler than the
earth that has been scorched

I ask all the questions, but the answers are all the same
Am I just a pawn to be used, like those still unwilling to
play the game
They snicker and sneer after every step I may take
Yet no decisions can be made that only I have the forti-
tude to make

I'll leave this journey and no wiser shall I become
Yet with the knowledge I gain, I leave my traces for the
young
Those that shall soon cross my path one day
Shall not have to look too far to find the truth in their
own unique and special way

Dreamed Reality

Disjointed looks and transient stares
You are heading off, yet not really sure as to where
All faces seem fuzzy and landmarks are askew
In some strange reality, this is truthfully your distinct
    point of view

You hear the voices of others so near
Yet the words that they speak don't resonate so clear
The people walk past, stuck in a world of their own
It's as if you are all together, yet still so all alone

They have their own lives, and on they do go
Not worried about their surroundings, or they don't seem
    to show
You roam in between them, they don't seem to care
To stop them for an instance, never shall you dare

To get an idea if all worries are completely the same
How will each person react, do none of them complain
Are any left with the fear of failing at life
In the shadows of darkness, do they ever fear the light

Is it only you who can't seem to just walk ahead
Crippled by doubt, remorse, and dread
Able to function though things aren't as they seem
Have you perfected your own lies, or is this only just a
    vivid distant dream

The people we cross on the streets each day
Are not really that different from those we know, or so
     we say
We all have demons trapped deep down inside
Afraid to release them, so with them we will hide

We do what we must, some flourish, while others will fail
Grasping for our own golden ship in which we set sail
Not letting life bother us, we march straight along
Knowing tomorrow shall become another yesterday that's
     gone

You are unable to skip through life without looking back
And those that stop for a moment are able to repel your
     past's attack
They have garnered all their strength and have conquered
     their past
So the only way to move now is toward a future that's
     built to last

The Trifecta We Win

As we reflect on all the things we have come to regret
We realize that life will never be considered a winning bet
We gamble on love, on happiness and what's right
We lose more than we win, yet still we bet it all to achieve
    what is there, out of our sight

Unable to imagine what fate has in store
So we throw more riches at it, never satisfied with having
    that much more
Some people waste what rightfully they have been given
Just to crawl on top of that mountain to witness how
    others are living

To see something better than what's there, in front of our
    own eyes
Wanting to acquire those items, to show that we don't live
    in our own disguise
We can't understand that life is made of the simple things
That bring us pleasure, despite never realizing the riches
    it brings

Some have fast cars or a mansion in the hills
Their joy becomes dampened when they notice they have
    lost life's thrills
Someone will come along with more fame and wealth
Jealousy will set in, it's identity covered in stealth

Live with what life will place before you
Achieve what you knowingly believe to be true
Your pockets may be full, but your heart sits there like an
    empty gas tank
The only thing you will have to show is a cup full of
    nothing from which you drank

Lay your bets on the table to wager on what you hope to
    achieve
Then you can gamble on those things, if only you believe
You can't use riches to gain what you truly desire
For in the end, your winnings come from love's endlessly
    burning fire

23 January 2016

Dried Tears

The water does flow, and no light shall shine
I only wanted what was never to be mine
Wishful dreams are all I had
I still can't believe it could have been all that bad

As I reached for the moon, I bypassed the stars
With tunnel vision, I just couldn't see what was so near
     and yet so far
I reached for what I chose for me
Now alone I sit here, realizing it was never meant to be

I had a plan of what it was that I could gain
Never fully understanding that what I wanted would only
     bring about pain
Blinded to consequences I never could tell
I left my soul to rot inside a self-created prison cell

To believe all that glistened could be held within my grasp
I placed on the blinders, unsure if it was meant to ever
     really last
As much as I desired for this wish to come true
I now know that dream should always have been to be
     with you

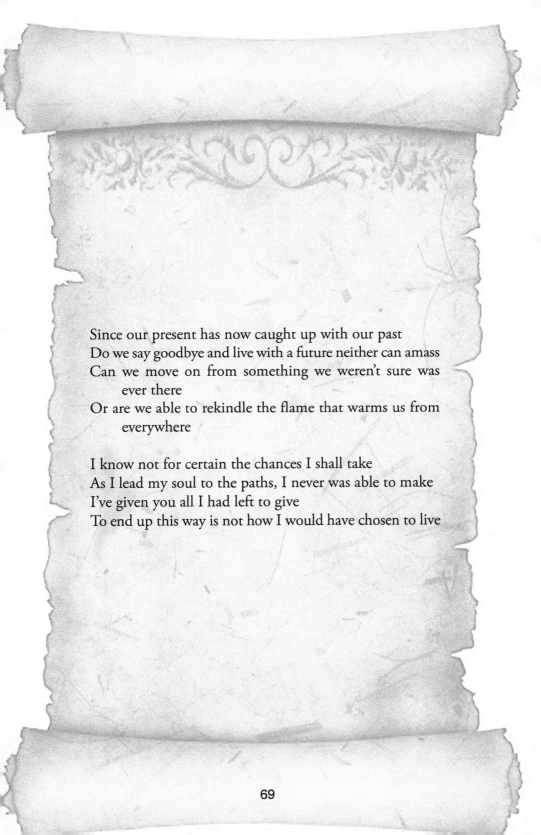

Since our present has now caught up with our past
Do we say goodbye and live with a future neither can amass
Can we move on from something we weren't sure was
    ever there
Or are we able to rekindle the flame that warms us from
    everywhere

I know not for certain the chances I shall take
As I lead my soul to the paths, I never was able to make
I've given you all I had left to give
To end up this way is not how I would have chosen to live

Fade from Black

Blackness, not the color, is all I see before me
Somehow the emptiness is suitable for us to see
To escape into nothing is our destiny it seems
To fight against it is useless, for you can't fight a dream

You can run around in circles and end up in the same place
It's the same as trying to fight out of an inescapable maze
Your way is soon lost, no savior to be found
All you really have left to do is put your boots on the
    ground

To slowly lighten up your way, you turn toward a darker
    gray
You can start to see the path that possibly leads to your
    escape
It's still not enough ambient light to brighten up the trail
So you must set forth and not be afraid to fail

The dimness will be the flicker of hope that you can seek
Don't fret over the loneliness, it only stands to make you
    weak
To lead yourself forward you have to take the very first step
It's then that you can conquer the fears that exhumes
    your breath

The dullness that emits from a stormy gray dawn
It's what shall greet you when your chances no longer
    seem to be gone

It's a light that barely shines to guide you toward a newer way
Only through your eyes shall you find the courage to never want to stay

The glistening of the morning sun, from streaks in the rain clouds
Seem to shimmer of hope for those whose life is no longer bound
To walk with a purpose, yet unsure as to knowing where
Just lift your eyes off the ground and straight forward you shall stare

Finally the whiteness of a new day's sun
The wind blows the clouds and the rain can no longer come
With each passing step, your journey grows much shorter than before
Suddenly it seems that you have grown stronger ever more

You may never overcome all the obstacles in the paths you do travel
But you have to fall sometimes to be scraped by life's gravel
The scars you will show will only make the ending that much better
For it leaves you reminders of all your troubles when finally you get settled

Seek your own way, the only way to know how
Learn from others and live in the now
When you feel those trials start to reattack
Remember how you overcame it before and you faded from black

Insurmountable

The odds are undeniable, or so I am told
With the vision I seek, may I one day behold
I give unto you, all I have left of me
Take what you will, I am whatever you see

I don't ever pretend to be what I am not
And in this convoluted world, you are all that I got
I give you my heart, the depths of my love
For one moment in time, our souls are bound from up above

Tightly wound together, intermingled with some fear
Your touch, your aura, draws me ever near
Forsaking the past while our future will continuously grow
My feelings and actions are all I have left to show

You have given me strength when I was at my worst
Every play we've taken is far from rehearsed
I speak to you with truthfulness and poise
Those who have doubted us are filtered out like back-
    ground white noise

I never gave up, though the chances were rare
That you and I could become what was never deemed fair
To pass this up had been entering into my thoughts
But I just couldn't relinquish a love with which I had sought

I promise to be the best you imagine I can
If you promise to take this broken soul as your own
    loving man

Decide for Yourself

You have but only one life to live
So how do you ration out the love that you give
Do you take the chance and give it all away
Or decide to hold a reserve for the proverbial rainy day

Is it fair to the one you are giving it to
When they begin to realize that you haven't been com-
    pletely true
You hold some back and they eventually will find out
Through your deception, you understand what pain is
    all about

You do know now that to withhold was wrong
You will pay for it in sorrow for so very long
You try to make up the difference, but they really don't
    seem to care
And you are left holding on to the hurt, showing on your
    face is true despair

If you were to give it all and they don't return it back
How are you to go forward with the will that you lack
You were taught to never leave anything to chance
To go headfirst and hold firm with your stance

So in your decision to leave nothing to luck
You went all in and now you're stuck
You've done what was right, so the choice now sits with
     them
If they want you right back, you can count that as your win

Which shall you choose, love partial or full
Time wastes no movement, to wait is to crawl
You gave what you could and hope it proves to be enough
To live this type of love makes life that much more rough

Awaiting the decision that they need to make
Your heart shall be theirs to leave or to take
You contemplate your choices while you count down the
     time
The situation is useless if you don't live a true loving life

6 August 2016

Multiple Dealings

Self-abuse is never healthy, and it really isn't that hard
It's not always physical but at times is written in the cards
You berate yourself mentally always within your head
No others will know that you continuously wish that
    your heart was dead

Think about this for just a moment, what good will it do
Except to relive all the years of pain stored deep inside you
Does it ever really go away, you tell yourself it will be so
But deeply set inside your mind you see the answer is no

So what can you do to rid yourself of this pain
You can smile all the time, but what possibly does that gain
The world won't know the difference, so why should they
    care
Yet they will be the ones to proclaim "Forever I'll be there"

You up and walk away for you know how bad it gets
You've been there before and the enemy you have met
Try to forget, it will conquer what's left of your mind
Never will it feel so good, it's not built to be so kind

Have another drink, it only causes you more harm
Then you will wake up sick as you hear the morning alarm
All that's left for you to do is to finally face it head-on
Then one day you will question, where could it all have gone

Living through Your Own Eyes

The young soul craves the danger
Afraid of nothing in his life
In taking risks, he is not a stranger
So he never has to question why

He goes through his existence
Hanging just off the edge
Refusing to accept the resistance
That others say will become his end

As he reaches his midpoint
And life weighs heavier on his mind
He still believes that he won't join
The people he wants to leave behind

He doesn't feel he has slowed down
As he tries to keep up with the youth
Yet the realization soon does make him frown
For he can't continue as he once would

The more mature he gets, the duller glows his flame
He knows he can't recover as quickly as before
He wants to continue on, yet he feels all his pain
As he learns someday soon, the will be no more

Once in a while he will attempt an old trick
To convince only himself that his fire is not gone
When it doesn't happen as easy as before, it makes him
     feel more sick
For it makes him realize that soon he will be done

He passes through his life remembering all his days
When nothing really mattered at all
Now he only has his memories within his mind to play
And he can smile at the visions of every single fall

When finally he rests and thinks of his past
He shows off his scars and gives a sly smile
He is proud of all he has done and forever it will last
Every scar is a journey throughout all of life's miles

The Roads We Make

As the day comes to a close and my mind goes astray
I can't help but wonder, could we have met in any possible way
Your life if busy, this I completely understand
But through my dire thoughts, I don't see myself in your demand

I sit here and ponder what it is you think about
While all the time trying to erase all my lingering doubt
I can't predict what it is the future will hold
But without an us, it only becomes more distinctly cold

For many a year we have been on this road
And like the pack mules of old, I carry this cumbersome load
Neither one of us knows what the other does think
Yet we keep coming back, like an alcoholic to a drink

Sacrifices are made, but is it ever enough
Through disappointment and sorrow, we both become more tough
Is the goal the same, are we on the right track
Or have our cars traveled too far to ever look back

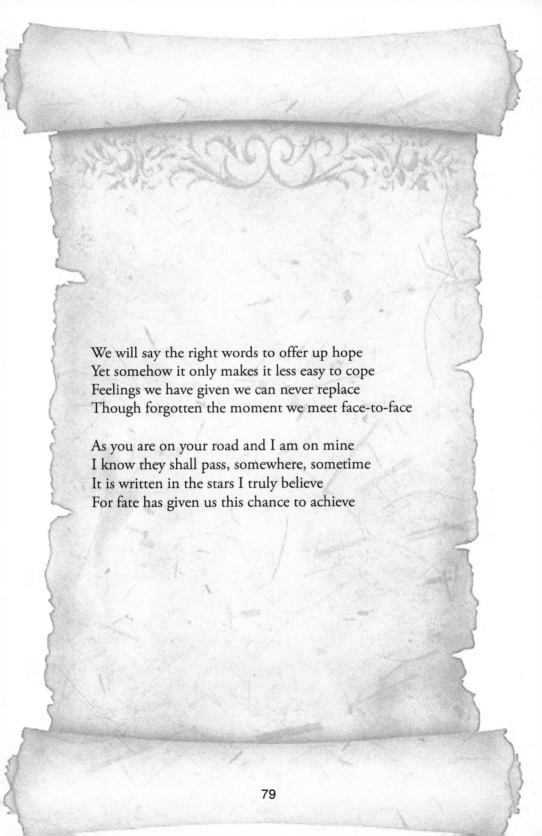

We will say the right words to offer up hope
Yet somehow it only makes it less easy to cope
Feelings we have given we can never replace
Though forgotten the moment we meet face-to-face

As you are on your road and I am on mine
I know they shall pass, somewhere, sometime
It is written in the stars I truly believe
For fate has given us this chance to achieve

Forever: Just a Dream

I strive to move forward, to only lose that ground
I scream into the night, yet I still don't make a sound
I try to become a little bit stronger
Yet my path only ends up being that much longer

I give without taking to no avail
And feel like I'm losing, no success, only fail
I can't win at all, no matter how hard I try
I sit here hanging my head, no ability left, I begin to cry

I seek what I will never be unable to comprehend
I will give up forever, is this to be our end
I put forth the effort to open your eyes so that you shall see
That this effort, with no compensation, is to be a reward
    for me

Do I only keep pushing forth to try
Or has that pushing given us a reason to finally say goodbye
Have I gone too forward to ever turn back
Is this because I display all you fear what I lack

Does it scare you with the thought that I might put all in
Do I know where this is about to begin
Can you provide me the results for all that I seek
Or have I started over in areas in which I show I am weak

Have you decided that this is a future you want
Or has this provided an out, that within your mind, I will
    forever haunt
I seek a finale I am bound to tread
Or am I to exit from something others have proclaimed
    is now dead

I shall never throw in the white towel to quit
Yet somehow if this is wrong, I realize this will be it
Shall we walk hand in hand toward our dying day
Or will I be secluded here now, with no words left that I
    can say

Twice Mistaken

I have made the same mistake again
The mistake was letting somebody else get in
I swore I would lock my heart's door for good
I guess it is something I knew I never could

I let her in because she showed that she cared
In the end it was me, the one who was scared
I don't think I will truly ever learn
Now in my head forever, her memory shall burn

I believed she was the one who could be for me
I cared so much I just couldn't see
That in the back of her head, she developed a plan
On how to destroy this vulnerable man

From this blow I shall never retrieve
The me you once knew, I honestly believe
She got what she wanted when she stole my heart
To think I was the one to enable this to start

Never again I will swear and mean it this time
No one will be allowed to commit that crime
Of stealing my heart and playing with my head
Instead of dealing with that kind of pain, I'd rather be dead

A Friend to the End

In a world filled with much sorrow and pain
I prefer to sit and watch the falling rain
When no one around seems to care
Open your eyes and you will see me there

When your world is starting to fall apart
Look deep inside what's left of your shattered heart
You will see, within you, a brighter, shimmering light
And in that glow you will witness a glorious sight
I will be standing there with open arms
To rescue you from all of your life's harms

You can count on me to be there until the end
Because I will be your closest friend
So when you are thinking you are bound to fail
Bring out a shovel along with a pail

Bury your troubles deep down in the sand
And grab hold of my extended hand
I'll show you what this life can be all about
With that, you will be able to shut all your troubles out

Beginnings and Endings

Ending of life, beginning of a new age
All you feel around you is misery and rage
Caught in a world no longer your own
So now the truth will finally be known

Take what you can, but leave all you get
For the truth is the only thing you will have met
Face-to-face with your demons inside
It's their rules to which you will soon have to abide

In the beginning there was a perfect life
In the end all that's left is you holding the knife
Laden with blood from the demon's eye
With that you set your soul free to fly

If you take my soul, I will gladly accept your pain
And walk around in misery through a steady, misting rain
I'll take advantage of what I see I can
Someday to die the death of a man

Ending of the old age, beginning of a new day
There is really nothing left for me to say
The trap has been sprung, and our lives are now set
With it is the happiness we will soon forget

A Fairy Tale

Elves and troll are dancing around
Another fairy tale recited without a sound
Demons astride dragons do also reside
Then in comes our hero, upon a stallion he does ride

A brave young lad in bright shining armor
His young lady awaits, imprisoned by those trying to
    harm her
He draws his sword within a blink of an eye
He points the tip toward the sky

Where witches do dwell and goblins will stay
In the middle of the forest where fairies will play
Darkness will shed its mysterious light
As evildoers do pray for the eternal night

The spells will be cast, and our hero will fall
Then the evil beings will rejoice and be proud of it all
Destruction and chaos shall soon overcome the land
So the fate of the world rests in our fallen hero's hand

Lightning will strike, and the thunder will roar
Suddenly an object appears on the shore
Our hero will arise and prepare for the impending war
To destroy that evil and settle the score

He will be victorious, and all will cheer
For the savior of the world is finally here
Goodness has won, so the people do shout
And this is what fairy tales are all about

A Day for Fools

Valentine's Day is made for those with true love
That's probably the reason my heart feels like a broken
    crystal dove
In a million tiny fragments scattered on the ground
So if you are looking, that's where it shall be found

I can't understand why life has to be so cruel
And why am I the one always chosen to play the part of
    the fool
You can never appreciate how that does make me feel
Only then can you understand how my pain is for real

They say there is somebody that's out there for you
But I am having my doubts that this statement is true
How long does one wait for that person to show
Because the hatred in my mind has started to grow

If you are out there, that someone who is meant for me
Why can't you show yourself so that I might see
This lifeless person whom they used to refer to as a man
Maybe you can restore the faith in me again

All along I have lived this life alone
So certain feelings were not free to have grown
Time is running out, this I do say
For the love I'm able to give on Valentine's Day

Battle of Wills

Long ago in a not-so-distant land
Lived a soldier, a warrior, a fighting man
A gladiator to fight this war on his own
A descendant of whom, it is really not known

Slaying his foes with a slash of his sword
His enemies do crumble like termite-ridden board
None shall he fear, invincible he may seem
But his deadliest adversary will appear out of a dream

Out of the shadows, the creature does appear
A pure vision of evil, it draws ever near
Stalking its prey with only one thing in mind
To seek out the warrior, to search, and to find

Suddenly spotted riding alone in the mist
No friends to call on, none around to assist
The battle he faces must be done on his own
Invincible or not, it shall soon be known

The fighting begins, yet no wounds can be seen
It's not a bloody battle and nowhere near fought clean
The battle is in his body, his mind and his soul
All are waiting to see who plays the victor's role

There will be no winners in the battle he has fought
The only victim, you could say, would be his pride that's
    now shot
He will emerge from the battle scarred but still brave
For there are things inside him that still he can save

Path of Life

Just take it one step at a time
For the road to forever is so hard to find
Take a look around before you go astray
Walk out too far and you will lose your way

There's only one path that you can take
Don't ask for help, it's your decision to make
Only you know where the truth will be found
Whichever path you take, you will forever be bound

Take it slow, there is no reason to be rushing along
Keep yourself going forward, and you will remain strong
Only you will be able to tell if it's the right path for you
If you won't tell me, let someone know what it is you are
    up to

When you finally decide which is your right path
Travel along it until your eternity is held within your
    grasp
Hold on to it tight and refuse to let go
Then, and only then, will you ever truly know

Vision of Paradise

A summer breeze blows softly through your hair
I still can envision you standing right there
Resting on the beach or standing on a mountaintop
The sight of you does make my heartbeat stop

Once in my arms, I won't let you go
I don't really care whoever will know
I walk proudly with you down the street
Another soul will we never meet

A vision of paradise has been delivered to me
Soon enough everybody around will see
Honestly how much in love we are
I know, once together, you will never stray far

A vision of paradise always in sight
I want to know if it's to last all night
You stay right here, never to go away
For I want you to always stay

You say you are mine, and I say I am yours
And you are the one I'll always adore
You look at me, and our eyes will lock
My heart then beats twice as fast as a clock

I tell you how beautiful it is you do look
Then I shall steal you away just like a crook
I take you straight to paradise
It won't matter the cost, I'll pay whatever price

You look like an angel just out of a dream
But can it be more real than what it does seem
We travel along toward a heavenly place
To take our minds off the rest of the human race

We can go if you will just say the word
Maybe then you can believe all that you have heard
Take to heart all the words that you do hear
For this love of ours has never been more clear

The Night

This is the night
This is the time that dreams were made of
This is the night
This is the place where we will fall in love

Nothing could destroy the plans you have set
From this moment on, we will never forget
All your fantasies that you keep inside
After tonight shall have no place left to hide

This is the night
This is the memory you are allowed to keep
This is the night
This is not a dream, and you are not asleep

All this magic is happening for you
Open your eyes and believe it is true
It's not make-believe, it's real what you see
Wrapped like a birthday present to you from me

This is the night
This is from the million stars sitting up in the sky
This is the night
This is us never having to ever say goodbye

Open Eyes

How can I continue to see her all the time
And not be able to tell her she's with the wrong guy
Why can't she just open her eyes to see
That the one meant for her just happens to be me

When she's having her problems, I'm the shoulder she
      cries on
I ask where he is, and she tells me he's gone
I comfort and protect her from any and all harm
By making her feel safe wrapped up in my arms

It's not that I mind the situation I'm in
But somewhere along the way, those feelings did begin
I try to stop them, but they just won't go away
I really can't mention them, what would I say
Excuse me, friend, I have developed feelings for you
She will avert her eyes, and I will know our friendship is
      now through

I will be back to where I have been before
I have almost lost a friend and so much more
I know my heart won't be able to take that again
I can't afford to have this good thing to end

So do I continue to keep my mouth shut
And bury my feelings like a bone from a mutt
Do I walk around with a smile and my head held high
Meanwhile my heart has begun to slowly die

I guess there's no choice about the road I must take
For I am used to feeling this heart of mine ache
I will recover from this as I have done in the past
I can't really state how much longer I will be able to last

Next time you see me, I will be the same person you know
A partial smile on my face and my courage I will show
I will help with your problems and be a great listening ear
Knowing that no matter what, it's always better having
      you right here

Evil Games of Mind

From the lateness of night to the earliest of morn
That's when you wake up and a new game is born
Those devious thoughts bred through your deepest dreams
Those mischievous thoughts and devilish schemes

Who shall I get to like me today
And then like the trash I will throw them away
I will give them a hope in which to hold on
Then in a blink of an eye, it soon shall be gone

You won't know what hit you, it's over so quick
But your memories of the moment, in your mind they
    will stick
I will leave you to deal with the pain I have caused
Off to the next to stick in my claws

I will succeed at this game forever, you can never win
For the master of the moment perfects the original sin
You can't have what you want, or that's what they say
I will prove it to you over and over again every day

I will toss out some bait, like a smile or a wave
And once you grab hold, I will take back what I gave
Keep you playing the fool in the game known as love
For it's in this matter you shall never rise above

Spring: Beginnings

Like flowers that bloom on the first day of spring
What wonderful tidings does the new sunrise bring
Is it something to fear
Like the loss of one so dear
Or the one present to give to make someone's heart sing

A day full of joy or a night filled with dread
Things that can get lost inside one's head
Be there to help you recall
Or to help you rise from the fall
The words you meant, but never have you said

Is it a symbol, a writing, or a sign
To show what may, or may not, be mine
Can you truly ever feel
Or has your imagination become more real
Isn't it time you crossed the unforeseen line

The promise of the day will soon be about to start
The eagerness that grows inside your heart
To anticipate that moment is your only goal
Yet to wait for that time can take its toll
Together for the moment and never should you part

The spring morning soon arrives when the sun does rise
To accept this time is the first step toward your prize
You can't escape destiny's trap
For within its wall you soon may snap
And be sent to sleep where you shall meet your demise

Awaken when your time is far from through
For when that moment comes, you shall know what to do
You take a step toward what you believe is right
It's not just the dreams you see in the night
For you shall know the truth is all I give to you

The light from the sunrise is soon to be above
The sounds from afar are the cries of a lonely dove
Within your heart it plants its seed
Only to grow in your time of need
And what shall materialize will be done when watered by
    one's true love

Nearing the End

Thinking back to when I was free
Nothing could be wrong as far as I could see
Suddenly enslaved by what I had not known
The cast is set, and my future is shown

Dealt to me by a withering hand
My very existence resting on the sand
Waiting to be plucked from within time's clutch
I only have to live, I do know this much

From out of the blue, my savior is here
They are coming into focus, yet still not that clear
Am I still dreaming, or is this for real
A human touch is all I really need to feel

The person is coming on so very fast
All I desire is for this vision to last
I will stay awake to see the light
Just remember that I won't leave without a fight

I will stick around and try to be brave
For somebody will come along and my life they will save

Being Alone

There is a boy who sits in a room
No light, no happiness, only gloom
On his face is displayed a stoic blank stare
When he is in the room, he's not really there

He made his world begin to crumble
And under his breath he starts to mumble
It's all my fault, I didn't know exactly what to do
I've had many a problem, yet no one ever knew

He never talked to anyone, so no one knew what was wrong
Did what he felt, in his mind, what was right all along
He thinks to himself that death would be great
But found out it wouldn't be before it was too late

So off to the hospital he commits himself to stay
he still sits there this very day
No one comes to visit, so it's painfully clear
That he is all alone in this place sitting here

When he finally dies, not a person will be sad
But I believe that he himself will be glad
Not a single tear will be shed upon his death
So with that in mind, he takes his final breath

Trapped

I feel as though I am trapped inside a square
When I look around, no one is there
This feeling reoccurs almost every night
But at the edges, I see the distant light

All I seek is someone to truly care
And with my feelings, they soon will share
I used to have someone like that
But with my feelings they crushed till flat

I wish they knew what that felt like
To have in your heart driven a spike
I might as well just give up now
In the fields of life, I'll play the plow

I will burrow through all the sorrow and hate
But in my mind, I see things as being great
No one will ever again know how I feel
To me, I will remember those feelings being too real

Next time you feel completely happy or glad
Think of me, but don't ever be sad
I will live to the fullest potential I can one day
Hoping to remember all the words I never could say

Something to Look Forward To

What's it like to have a dream
Only to have it torn right at the seam
What's it like to be forced to see
Someone you care about up and flee

There is not much that we are able to do
To adjust the past that we did live through
So we must live from day to day
Each morning, get up and start to pray

Pray that things will turn out right
At the end of the tunnel, hope to see the light
If you see a dream begin to fade away
Let it go, let it fly astray

Another will come along, this I promise you
This is something I believe to be true
You can't live your life dwelling in past mistakes
And with the rest of your dreams you apply the brakes

Go on someday and you shall reach the top
With your new goal, you never will stop

Denial

I see the truth deep within your eyes
Amidst the shadows, the clouds, and the lies
The feelings there are more than real
Not something easy for others to steal

Look deep in your soul and you can tell
This is something you are unable to pawn or sell
Keep on trying if you think you must
But this mission of yours, will soon be a bust

Give up now, for you can never win
As much as you try to stop it, the feelings still sink in
It's useless to avoid this I continue to say
I'll repeat the same to you every single day

The thing I speak of, comes from somewhere above
The poets have a word for it, I believe it's love
I know it's something you just can't handle
But it burns in us all like an infinite candle

Continue to try, I soon won't care
Take a look inside, but please don't stare
What you see may scare you a bit
Only then can you realize that this is truly it

Beach Memories

Sitting on the beach in the glistening sun
Watching those around you having their fun
Playing in the sand, maybe catching a wave
Memories like this are the ones you want to save

Walking around and collecting shells buried in the sand
Holding them tightly within your hand
Building a castle to reach to the sky
And staring at the birds above your head they do fly

When it's time to go, you struggle to leave this place
It was so much fun, being here in your own space
With so much room to move around
The ocean was the only thing to create a somber sound

Change Promised

Standing at the ocean, staring at the waves
Thinking back on all my better days
I used to have fun under a brightened sky
Now I live in the gloom and wonder why

She would come to me like out of a dream
It was the reality of it, or so it did seem
Then she disappears out of my sight
And I am left standing there, so I turn out the lights

I just want back what once was mine
To make my life be perfectly fine
If you are to hear these words, come back to me
Things will get better, I will guarantee

I want to change, your help is what I seek
It may take an hour, a day, or even a week
I need you here, by my side through it all
Then life will be easier if you just make that call

Future Shock

As I walk through this life, I think of what I could be
But the future envisioned truly does scare me
I'm not quite sure what it is I will do
I only know my thoughts are to be with you

If given the chance to make a wish
A chance like that I shall not miss
I want to live a genuine happy life
Without having to go through all troubles or strife

Most people will not be able to firmly grasp
The costliness of mistakes they have made in the past
Those errors come back to haunt us one day
There's nothing about it that you can say

We will have to try to make it through
To bring into our lives something new
Don't try to escape what it is you don't know
For it is with you wherever you will go

You cannot run, nor are you able to hide
From the little voices you hear within your mind
It could be danger or a trusted friend
But it's there with you until the very end

My future right now seems to be dull and bleak
And my future is now, no time to be weak
I'll face it head-on as bravely as I can
One day I will be able to call myself a man

What's the Difference

As I continuously walk down these well-worn streets
I try to figure out why my life feels so incomplete
It's then I realize that I am missing you more
Than I ever imagined I could before

So what's the difference if I am a mess
Things are the same, more or less
Who's gonna care if I cry in the dark
As I walk listlessly alone inside the park

My life could be better, though not much worse
I still feel that I am stuck under your curse
I don't really mind not knowing what to do
I'll learn to live my life knowing it's now without you

What's the difference if I'm not there
No one will notice, nor do they ever care
What will it matter if I am all alone
If it stays as it is, no chance will I have blown

I'll keep to myself, no harm will be done
Maybe one day, I will find that perfect one

Captive

Here I'm stuck with this ball and chain
Left outside in the pouring rain
My heart was tied into a knot
Left alone to start to rot

You are the one who has the key
To set this broken heart of mine free
Instead you feel you have the need
To sit there waiting for me to beg and plead

I am stuck in a make shift jail
Can't afford to pay the bail
The prices I pay are way too high
So can you at least set my soul free to fly

I can't handle being held captive every night
It is like not having the ability to fight
You are the master, I play your slave
As hard as I try, I am unable to be brave

Set me free so I may go
To that beautiful garden where the flowers will grow
I am your prisoner, it seems, for life
So remove my heart with your unsharpened knife

I no longer need it, can't you see
Because your love is the key
To set this lonely captive free

Changes

Anger and frustration well up inside me
But pain and misery are all I see
Destruction to myself is all I can do
To cope with these problems I can't see through

The pain in my life is not as clear as it may seem
Sometimes I wish that it was only a dream
To help me break through my own living hell
By dropping this heart of mine into the deepest of wells

I feel as though I will give up one day
Then with my life they can throw away
Because there's not much left, of that I'm sure
Then I can live somewhere different forevermore

If I could go back in time and change it all
I would do it in a flash and build that wall
To block out the pain that's set to exist
No matter how hard I attempt to resist

I will stand up and fight like a man
To change from my worst to the best that I can
I will acquire the ability to fight again
Only then will my real life truly begin

4 January 1993

Your Biggest Day

As you walk down the aisle, you begin to reminisce
About the life you had and the things you will miss
The freedom to go wherever you choose
Without leaving behind someone you could possibly lose

You look ahead, a bright future you do see
With someone you love beside you for all eternity
Someone to comfort you when you are feeling down
And that someone in your arms as you go through your
     town

This is the day you will remember for all your life
Whether you are the husband or the wife
Your wedding day is special for just you two
For your new life begins with those two little words— "I do"

Fork in the Road

Churning and burning, your life is a mess
Perfection in the world is what you obsess
Drawing a pattern in your mind
Slowly but surely you fall behind

Living in the past is safe and way too much fun
Striving for a future is the difficult one
Make the choice to stay where you are
Then a happiness you seek will not be that far

If you choose to move your life ahead
Chances are good, you will wind up dead
Left to rot on a cold, empty street
Recognizable only by the scars on your feet

The choice is yours and only yours to make
Your decision could put your life at stake
Stay safe where you are, most likely to live on
Take the chance to go forward and life as you know it
    may soon be gone

Unrevealed Secrets

Recalling the events from your past
Searching for those you are sure will last
Tossing aside the ones that hurt you the worst
So those that remain are free from your curse

Good intentions are what you shall perceive
And this is all you wish to believe
The truths you hide will be exposed one day
But until then, it's the lies you continue to say

Freedom at last from memories within
Now your new life can really begin
Your secrets came out, and no one seemed to care
On to better things, you will go from there

Secrets

I'll never tell how I feel
Because then I won't believe it's real
If anyone found out the truth about me
They would understand how I live in misery

I have to hide as long as I can
For everyone has to see this fictitious man
If they like the unreal one
The true one can then hide away from the fun

His vision is gone forever from view
No matter how hard he tries, it's impossible to break
    through
He will keep his silence forevermore
And on this part of my life, I shall lock that door

12 August 1993

Facing the Truth

Silence is golden, or so they say
So why is the truth so hard to keep away
Why do I feel like I need to shout
And tell you what my hell's all about

I need to explain how it is I do feel
To trust you enough to know it's real
Will you throw it back in my face
Or take it to heart, for then it has found its place

I want to know if you will play with my mind
Are you really that vicious kind
Will you then play with my head
Because if you do, I'd rather be dead

I don't need this thrown back at me
The consequences are something you won't want to see
Everything I've worked for will have been for not
And the happiness I've gained, I will soon have forgot

Can We Talk

Why is it when I call you
You always have an excuse
You do not know what you put me through
When you turn me loose

There is so much that I have to say
If you will give me a chance
Then you up and turn me away
And perform your goodbye dance

Open your eyes just a little bit
Then maybe you can see
That what I have to say is really it
And it's meant for you from me

One more time is all I ask
So may I please have a turn
I will then take off this phony mask
Maybe from this you will finally learn

The words I say have been kept inside
Because they were just too difficult to tell
I figured out it was best to just hide
And not bring you into my personal hell

Life's a Beach

Left there lying on the rocks
Trying to deal with your own hard knocks
Suddenly washed upon life's shore
Your troubles drift off forevermore

The tide comes in and then goes away
Never will it be able to stay
It is like the people we come to know
In the blink of an eye, away they will go

Shifting through the sand with your feet
Each grain represents the people you meet
The ones that care throughout everything will stick
The others drift off with a simple flick

As you watch the waves go rolling by
A lonely tear falls from the corner of your eye
It quietly dries up as you watch the sun set
And away goes another person you have met

A Journey for Life

A trip bound for nowhere
Is where I am headed to
Knowing that you may be there
Just helps me to get through

The journey that I'm on won't be very long
But then, it won't be quick
I know this definitely can't be wrong
So with this plan, I promise I will stick

When I reach the end, it may be the right place
Then again, maybe it won't be
I'll only know if I see your face
So I guess I'll have to wait and see

This trip to nowhere has already begun
Aimlessly traveling in a roundabout way
Knowing that you will always be the one
Is all the incentive I need to forever stay

27 August 1994

Immortality

Immortality, you give your all
Waiting patiently for its call
Living forever upon this earth
To never die in the land that gives us birth

You always hope you are the one
To be regarded as the earth's chosen son
To live off the land and always be free
As close to perfection as you could possibly be

Roaming around with new places to go
Through sun, wind, and even the snow
Absorbing what all you can from this place
Never really sure if you are the last of your race

Live like you want, for you are sure it's okay
Never live for tomorrow, but only for today
Remember your fate is in someone else's hand
Now you are free to roam forever within this promised
    land

Enemy?

Watch them tumble, then they fall
If you're lucky, you'll hit them all
It will come if you give it time
One more minute and it will be mine

Patience truly is the key
To cut the gap between you and me
I will break down that wall of pain
And use those bricks for my own gain

Every stone you toss will be used to fight
The unforeseen villains that stalk you all night
Surely they will come, but we know not when
I do know for a fact, so I repeat it again

Be prepared for this battle and the upcoming war
If you are lucky, you will wake up and go back for more
You will battle until the bitter end
Then the only one remaining will be your true friend

I Just Need Time

Sitting alone feeling nothing but remorse
I can't remember any time in my life that I have felt worse
I hate being here knowing that you are there
After hearing you say that you just don't care

You truthfully can't mean the harsh words you spoke
In the heat of the moment, your heart felt broke
You spoke without giving it too much thought
And by letting you know this, maybe more time I have
    bought

I need the time to reverse those words
That in my heart I have never heard
I need more time to change your mind
So we can leave those words behind

Another day, though not the same
You are in a crowd and call out my name
I hear an echo from across the way
And I turn to listen to what you have to say

Come back to me so we can start anew
I was foolish and didn't know what to do
Is that why there is sadness in your eyes
Or is there another reason for those soft little cries

22 July 1995

Just Like Yourself

Life on the run with nowhere to go
No place for your face ever to show
Your reputation has always followed you around
From the biggest cities to the smallest towns

You've always been known to play the fool
From your days as a baby and all the way through school
You'd love to change, but not sure how
So you try to hide within another crowd

Everyone you meet says, "Go away, young man"
You attempt to devise a new master plan
You will show them you are different from all the rest
And one day you prove you're simply the best

It will take some time to change thoughts in their heads
Most times, it happens well after you're dead
They will say things most just won't mean
Just think in life, you lived in your own dream

Your Heart's Roads

Your heart can go down three different roads
But the most important was the one you chose
It doesn't matter which one you would take
For eventually you will see, it was all a mistake

The road that goes up leads straight to your brain
It is the one that keeps you from going insane
It justifies your thoughts and leads you straight
Some feel this path really isn't that great

The next road to choose will lead you down
It stops at your feet and leads you through town
To carry you down a lonesome long street
Hoping wherever you stop is where you should be

The last road to go leads straight to your soul
Where life and happiness are free to grow
You don't really know where you should turn
But wherever you choose, your love will forever burn

Choose the roads you feel is right
Whichever you choose, love isn't that far out of sight
Whether you go up, down, or deep inside
From love, there never is a true place to hide

14 August 1995

By Your Side

Have you ever felt such a crippling fear
That leaves you wishing someone was near
To hold your hand as you start to cry
And wipe those tears from your eyes

To hold you close and never go away
They'll always know exactly what they should say
To be by your side on all those lonely nights
And tell you everything will be all right

To help you to never be that scared again
To let you know, you'll forever have a friend
Always be there through the good and the bad
And all the times you're happy or sad

Saying Goodbye

Thinking back to a time when
I thought I lost a friend
I turned around and saw you near
But the problem remained is, you weren't here

Take me back to the time that I
Had so much hope, but too little pride
Bring me back to who I once was
My life in unclear, a constant fuzz

I want to hear about the day I died
Not my body, but my heart inside
Take my pain so far away
Give me the words I am unable to say

I know you understand that this is real
But you just can't tell me how I should feel
Unto you I leave all that I can give
But now I know I can no longer live

My life the way it used to be
Without someone who is just for me
You go your way, and I'll go mine
Never to meet again in time

Our separate roads shall never cross
And this is where I will suffer my loss
One day, we will meet on the other side
It's then I'll say my final goodbye

Impossible Love

She says its forbidden, this love that you feel
Nothing can happen, it seems so unreal
You're supposed to ignore the words from your heart
Because all you envision just can't ever start

You spill your guts and hope she will respond
But after hearing your words, you look and she's gone
You now feel lost, your world starts to spin
You're turned inside out, so where to begin

Impossible love is what you have they all say
An impossible love that won't go away
Try as you must, you shall never see
A love for you that's not meant to be

What makes it impossible, how did I go wrong
I must not let her know, I shall remain strong
On the outside, I'll show the clown that I am
Joking and laughing the best that I can

On the inside I'll have a different story to tell
I'm burning in the fires of my self-made hell
I only want to die, to forever leave this place
To rid myself of the memories of her beautiful face

This impossible love shall remain untrue
No matter the feeling I will harbor for you

A Battle for Naught

Darkness lies over the fields tonight
For none are left to continue this fight
No one can claim this fight to be won
For no one is left to hold their gun

The massacre began shortly after dawn
And it continued throughout the whole day long
Surrender was not a word to enter their head
So all that fought have wound up dead

This war was right, or so they thought
Day and night they continuously fought
A fight for what, we shall never really know
The questions we have are left here to grow

No one is the winner, for they all have lost
They all paid the price, not knowing at what cost
Their bodies will lie in a man-made grave
And what we have learned, just isn't worth enough to save

Fight your battles if you believe in what it's for
So when you die, you will have settled your score
Don't go in not knowing what to do
Or the next one we find could end up being you

She's Not You

When I take a look into another's eyes
It's only then do I realize
That she's not you

I try my best to dismiss that fact
And look for things that she does lack
But still the thought comes racing through
The truth still remains is that she's not you

She's not you
Nor will she ever be
She's not you
You're the only one I see
She's not you
No matter how hard I try
She's not you
The thought will never leave my mind

I try to look the other way
When other girls come out to play
They'll never replace what I had in you
So what else is there for me to do

I can't forget what once was there
But trying to move on gives me a scare
I don't think that I ever could
And I don't know if I ever would

She's not you
Nor will she ever be
She's not you
You're the only one I see
She's not you
No matter how hard I try
She's not you
The thought will never leave my mind

I'll take these memories to the grave
For they are the things I shall have to save
Believe the words I speak, for they will ring true
There can never be another like you

Break Out

With the barriers they set, you must break through
You know it's something you have to do
With no force, you have to crack their wall
Don't ever give up, give it your all

You must reach inside and touch their soul
For winning it over is the ultimate goal
Stand strong and don't give up without a fight
Your willpower can conquer all her might

Keep pressing on but ease back on the force
Straight to her heart is your predestined course
It's gonna be rocky and rough at times
But the peak is the spot to where you must climb

Keep going forward no matter what she may say
For it's part of the game that she likes to play
Eventually you reach the end of the road
Then it's your job to carry the burden of her load

When you finally reach the end
You'll discover the heart of a lifetime friend

Just a Friend

Why do fools fall so fast
Knowing soon that they will crash
I gave my heart and soul to you
Much too quickly to know what you should do

I tried to change up that choice
But along the way I lost my voice
Never able to speak the words I feel
Now the situation is much too real

You say you want to be just a friend
Those words shall haunt me to my end
I've heard that phrase too many times
I think it's tattooed in my mind

I would like to store that phrase on a shelf
But I know I'll hear it again from someone else
It will bring back that reoccurring pain
One that hurts so much it drives you insane

I want to stop the cycle I'm stuck inside
For once in my life, I'd like to feel loved
Being a friend was great in the past
Back when love didn't exist, and a friendship could last

Trying to Prove It

A second chance to start all over again
To make you believe there is no end
To do what I must from the start
To give you everything, with all my heart

To let you know, no secrets will I keep
So cast aside your fears and lie by me to sleep
Your dreams are as wonderful as they may seem
For they will turn into reality, this I can guarantee

Nothing will be as it was before
No skeletons in my closet, nothing to ignore
Honesty and truth, I say you will know
For lies won't have the chance to grow

Someday soon I'll make you understand
This is no scheme, I have no great master plan
I lay my cards on the table in front of you
There is no hidden agenda that you can't see through

Open to you always is my heart's door
So don't slam it close forevermore
Give me a second chance so that I can prove
That I won't play that game, and onward we can then move

A Helping Hand

Like telling a baby bird it's time to fly
They'll never question the reason why
It's something they realize that they must do
And in their special way, they will always thank you

You must go when mother earth gives you her call
But never fear, she won't let you fall
She'll hold you tight and never let go
This is something that deep down inside you know

Trust all you can for she knows what's right
Don't bother to struggle, no need to fight
Let yourself go, she will take control
Forever with her, you shall remain standing tall

Only with peace shall you now rest
In all your life, she has shown you the way to be your best
She continues to guide your path until the end
Always by your side, like a loyal and true friend

She'll never leave you nor lead you astray
She is here forever, never will she go away
Mother earth is there until you do rest at last
The end comes near, though you don't know how fast

When you feel your time at last has come
Feel joy for she was with you when your life on earth is done

Take Me Away

I need you now, come take me away
To a place where our heart will be free to play
A place where our feelings, we shall never have to hide
To a place where I know you're always by my side

Take me somewhere we will be free to roam
A place we can live and to call our own
Somewhere no one has ever been before
A place that's ours forevermore

Take me away never to return
Where we can watch the world around us burn
Take me away, just get up and go
A place where our love will forever grow

Take me away and never look back
And as we leave, I'll cover our tracks
Can you take me so that you can see
All the things we have felt were so meant to be

Can you take me now and forget the past
And remember always that our love will last
Let's just go and find the trail
Like ships on the sea, we will set sail

We go away to start all over again
Once we take that first step, that's how we begin
Take me away never to return
Where we can watch the world around us burn

Take me away, just get up and go
A place where our love will forever grow
Take me away and never look back
And as we leave, I'll cover our tracks

Take me away, take me today
Take me away, no words are needed for us to say
Let's just go, I'll follow your lead
For that look in your eyes is all I'll ever need

Dream Kept Alive

Was there ever someone you so desperately wanted to meet
Someone so magical that they swept you off your feet
Someone so dynamic you couldn't believe your eyes
And the fact that they notice you is the biggest surprise

Have you pictured this person beside you wherever you go
That everything they've done is replayed like an old TV
    show
You know everything there is to know about her
If she can ever be yours, you are not really sure

When you fall asleep at night, it's only her you do see
From the length of her hair to her unforgettable beauty
You remember the touch of her hands as she is holding
    yours
That feeling is something never felt by you before

Can something so dreamlike ever really happen in your life
Where the girl of your dreams one day will become your
    wife
You picture this moment with every breath that you make
It's then that you realize it's all a mistake

Only something this wonderful could happen in a dream
If it looks to be this grand, it will never be as real as it
    does seem
So keep your dreams in your head where they do belong
And maybe someday, the *one* will finally come along

Say How You Feel

When you start to worry
Your heart becomes real still
Though you wish that time could hurry
You know you will wait for that thrill

You always time things so right
So the feeling doesn't end
But when others come within sight
Finished or not, your thoughts you send

It may not be what you really want to say
The words you say will still ring true
But you still rush it out anyway
And hope the message somehow comes through

Your thought become scrambled within your mind
You see things, but they don't seem all that clear
You try to leave those things behind
And you listen but never really hear

When speaking about feelings that come from the heart
The words you speak are only yours
From out your mouth the words do part
Your mind decides when to lock the doors

Your mind knows what needs to be said
It will stop it when you've made your point
Though now the moment seems to be dead
Your heart and mind will soon be joined

Friend

After all we've been through, we still do talk
To me, that means more than a moonlight walk
We give it our best and give it our all
But sometimes the bad trips us up and we fall

We've both been through a lot, yet we both do know
That through that pain, it makes our friendship grow
If you need an ear, I'm always here for you
And I know that you will do the same for me too

We may disagree about the things the other has done
The choices we made aren't always the logical ones
We'll have our troubles, like we have had in the past
But yet we see that our friendship is built to last

I appreciate the times when you put up with me
Through so much hurt, I just couldn't see
Why you didn't give up and tell me to go
Why you cared so much, I'll never truly know

Of the times you hurt me, I cannot tell
And all the ways that I know I put you through hell
I never gave up because I know the real you was there
I wouldn't ever walk out, I will always care

I hope you will be there until the very end
For me you will always be that one special friend

You Can Never Go

I thought when you left the music would die
But now you're gone, it continues to play, I don't know why
Maybe you weren't the one who was meant for me
If you aren't, then tell me why it couldn't be

I thought the stars were placed in the sky for just us
Because you were the one that I could always trust
But somehow my plans were different than yours
You traveled off on your own, set about on a different course

Suddenly that fork appeared in our road
So off we traveled, we burden our own load
Maybe one day our roads will once again be crossed
Then we will travel on together, forgetting the time we
        had lost

I don't want to give up on all I have ever known
For it's something that both of us can see has now grown
I couldn't stand to watch it all wither away
If there is still a chance it could live if you would only stay

Give it some time for things to straighten themselves out
Then you could understand all that I am talking about
If you take off without even giving it a try
For the first time in your life, you will witness me cry

You will be the only one that I will forever live for
And if you were to go, then there will be no more
No one could replace what I know I have in you
No matter what they say or they ever try to do

Remember these words when you fall to sleep at night
For others will come to try to steal your light
As hard as they may try, they will fail to win your heart
Because you will realize the we aren't meant to be apart

Subtle Changes

I know some of the words that I do say
May not always come out in the proper way
I know my actions may seem to be cruel
It's only because I am such a fool

I'm doing the best that I can
To stop being such a bitter man
It will not happen overnight
So please understand this, I don't want to fight

I only want everything to be perfect for you
In all I say, I will show and do
What you mean to me, it's hard for me to tell
Maybe then, it's just as well

Please have the patience to let me deal with this
I promise this old me you shall never have to miss
You will be surprised how much I have changed
Then what I do now won't seem to be so strange

Maybe in the end, it will all work itself out
And you will know what I am talking about
Hopefully, with my changing, you can then change your
     mind
So we may now leave the dark past behind

Show Remorse

You can't take it back, what you have done to me before
It doesn't have that effect on me anymore
All that's in the past will have to stay there
For now I know that you no longer seem to care

One thing I know for sure is that I cannot stay
And from this moment on, I will have nothing more to say
The way I was treated was really not that fair to me
But you were too blind to look and see

Everything that ever mattered, you tossed aside
From this guilt you can no longer hide
Try as you must, I refuse to play your game
And between us you know it will never be the same

Go off on your own, but soon you will realize
That you will never catch me with tears in my eyes
I will go on to find something new
Thankfully, that person will never be you

You will walk in the room, and I turn to see you stare
I will never show how much I ever did care
I'll turn back around and look in her face
And the mental pictures of you I have all but replaced

Since this is the end, I do wish you the best
Always remember it was you who started this mess
Show some responsibility for all that you have done
Before everyone you ever cared about is suddenly gone

New Man

Now that you're gone, I'm finally free
To live for myself, to live just for me
All things I ever did were just for you
The thanks you gave didn't seem to be true

I can live how it is I want to now
But at this moment, I really don't know how
I need to make changes and make sure I do it right
Even though I do know that it won't happen overnight

So now that you have left and I am all alone
What can I do now that you are gone
Can I live for myself in every way
And if you come back, what will I have to say

I'm not quite sure how it is I will react
If you make that decision to finally come back
Will those memories of old arise again
And will we be able to only be friends

I understand you did what you thought you had to do
I do want you to know that I'll always care about you
After the moment you said goodbye
I wiped those tears out of my eyes

I have finally dealt with all the pain
and cried my tears without the rain
I have moved on to a much better place
To once again rejoin the whole human race

If the day should ever come
When I see your face shining in the sun
I will say hello, and you will do the same
But know this time, I refuse to play your game

The End of it All

It's the strongest thing I've ever felt
I scream out loud for someone's help
No one comes to be by my side
Now there is no place for me to hide
Can someone help me out of this mess I'm in
I don't remember how it all begins
Suddenly I am back in a familiar place
Someone is there, yet I can't see their face
Is it a friend or possibly a foe
That's something I guess I'll never know
Just when I thought I couldn't take anymore
I feel death knocking on my door
The end is near, I feel it's chill
He's coming back for life's latest kill
I try to speak, no words come out
Never am I to know what this is all about

First Kiss from Love

They say you always remember your first love's kiss
And when they leave, it's all that you will miss
Someday I would like to have that chance
To be caught inside that magical trance

To feel your velvet lips softly touching mine
I only know that it is a matter of time
As I run my fingers across your cheek
This is the opportunity I so desperately seek
To hold you forever in my arms
To provide you security from all that will cause you harm

As our lips meet, the magic does start
A sensation both of us feel deep within our hearts
The time will slowly drift away
There are no words we should ever need to say

I want to feel that sensation with you
I have to know, is what they say true
The gentle compassion that we will feel
Not from a peck on the cheek, but a kiss that is real

Gotta Get Out

There is a place that I must go
That place is where I will not be known
The place to where I can always shine
A location that I can finally call mine

A far-off place that's miles from here
A town that knows not of my fears
One where I can start all over again
A place that's where I have never been

I see this place every night in my dreams
I only hope it will be real, much more than it seems
I can start anew and not have to worry
Will things go right for there is no hurry

The place is here now before my very eyes
A place I have seen a thousand times
It's finally there and will never be gone
This place is where I can call my home

Maybe One Day

How about for once you let the nice guy win
That's the way it should have always been
He shouldn't be the one to always finish last
It's that notion in life you should all get past

The nice guy is the one who always get pushed around
Taken advantage of and kicked to the ground
You know if you need it, he will be there for you
So you take advantage of him and toss him aside when
      you're through

You make him believe he is worth a lot
But what you can't see is that he knows he is not
He understands his position in life he is in
Afraid to say no, for it could mean the loss of friends

That is the fear he lives with every day
He's scared to tell you that he's always felt that way
So he goes through life like a welcome mat
To do this for you and also do that

The nice guy one day will break through his shell
He'll get what he deserves and treat it so well
He won't treat others as they have treated him
And in the end he knows that for once, he will win

Your Choice

I need to know if you are ready to set me free
So that I can finally start to really be me
It's obvious to all I'm not what you need
So if that's the case, let my heart go, I will plead

I have never wanted to let you go
But the way you have been acting, I need to know
Do you want me involved in your life
Someday to have you forever as my wife

I can't continue like this for too much more
It's breaking my will and spirit, I know this for sure
You need to decide if I am to let you be
To live the life that will be destined without me

I'm such a mess within my head
Those are the facts and my biggest dread
I fear for what I will become
Without you here, all I feel is numb

Make your decision and please make it fast
If you want what we have, for eternity, to last
You need to choose if it is me that you want
And not just to tease and not to taunt

I've fallen down into the darkened abyss
For it is you that I shall always miss
Is this finally going to be the end
And what of my heart, to you, I did lend

I want to see your face with my own eyes
Or is your happiness you portray just a disguise
Do you want me as your man
To take me just as I am

Choose soon and make this real
Or no longer with your love shall I ever feel
If your choice is not me, then let me go
Release my heart that you keep in tow

You're attached to me from all that we have been through
Yet I have no idea as to what I need to do
If you make the choice to forget the memories we share
I'm letting you know that forever I will care

I'm getting older, or can't you tell
And soon with my heart, I won't even be able to sell
I won't want to approach another girl
Without thinking of how you're still in my world

Make the decision that will be right for you
Just let me know what it is you want me to do
Please make your choice before my soul should die
Or leave me here with the tears from an angel cries

A Play

I think today I shall write a play
And then I will play the part
Of a man that suffers on this day
A tragic broken heart

I will play this part, if you shall please
I will start it off this way
It won't be done with the greatest of ease
But it shall be finished by the end of this day

This man will cry a thousand tears
Over the loss of the girl of his dreams
He would much rather face his biggest fears
Than to hear her rejecting screams

She will be the one he will always think about
Each and every single day
It makes him then have to scream and shout
But still end up by running away

This play will wind up to be a tragedy
I believe this to be true
I know from your eyes that it's plain to see
But there is really nothing that we can do

So think of this play as you live out your life
Then you won't ever have to act out the part
Of the man who suffers on this day a fragile, shattered
    heart

One Question Left Unanswered

Life is but a state of mind
And the meaning of it you shall never find
Try as you must though you will see
The answer to the question may never be

Living on the earth isn't always that great
And it is the living you will soon learn to hate
Knowing how to love since the day you were born
But learning to hate is what they do scorn

Questions will come about and then they will go
And the answers to those you shall never know
You will search for them until the end of your time
But life is like a mountain you are unable to climb

I looked for the answers while it was a must
But the quest I started on turned into a bust
I will now leave the earth, never to return
So may the answers to life someone someday learn

Costly Mistake

Standing on the outside glancing in
You start to think about all that could have been
If only you could change all the wrong done in the past
A true love relationship is what would be yours at last

So you said some things you didn't really mean
The real you was exposed and that's all they had seen
You can never take back the words that you say
And because of that, they never look at you again in the
    same way

Feelings get hurt much too easily, it does seem
That you wish you were living in a world full of dreams
Then you could erase the mistakes and try to make it right
Just so you won't end up alone in bed each and every night

Living just isn't the easiest thing that you will ever do
Be careful not to make mistakes that will come back to
    haunt you
Expectations of others are most times too great
Think first and be on the inside with love and not outside
    with hate

The Reality

Take me for what I am, not for what I could be
Life's doors will not always slam
For once they will open for me
The spirits there will overcome
All the evil in my life
This may not be true for some
For love is like an nonsharpened knife
Things are now better
Than they have ever been before
Though it really doesn't matter
Because you are mine now forevermore
Just remember the words that I have to say
And know all them to be true
That time on from this day, I am here just for you

About the Author

Shawn P. Lehto was born and raised in Torrance, California, and resides in Redondo Beach, California. In his free time, he loves to fish and golf. He is also a football (Raiders), hockey (Kings), and baseball (Angels) fan. He works as a driver in the aerospace industry.

CPSIA information can be obtained
at www.ICGtesting.com
Printed in the USA
FSHW011506030219
55416FS